MARTIN COUNTY LIBRARY SYSTEM, FL

JUL 1 0 2006

Places in American History

Jamestown

by Frances E. Ruffin

Reading consultant: Susan Nations, M.Ed., author/literacy coach/consultant in literacy development

WEEKLY WR READER®
EARLY LEARNING LIBRARY

Please visit our web site at: www.earlyliteracy.cc
For a free color catalog describing Weekly Reader® Early Learning Library's
list of high-quality books, call 1-877-445-5824 (USA) or 1-800-387-3178 (Canada).
Weekly Reader® Early Learning Library's fax: (414) 336-0164.

Library of Congress Cataloging-in-Publication Data

Ruffin, Frances E.
    Jamestown / by Frances E. Ruffin.
      p. cm. — (Places in American history)
    Includes bibliographical references and index.
    ISBN 0-8368-6410-7 (lib. bdg.)
    ISBN 0-8368-6417-4 (softcover)
    1. Jamestown (Va.)—History—17th Century—Juvenile literature. 2. Virginia—History—Colonial
period, ca. 1600–1775—Juvenile literature. I. Title.
    F234.J3R84 2006
    975.5'4251–dc22   2005026267

This edition first published in 2006 by
Weekly Reader® Early Learning Library
A Member of the WRC Media Family of Companies
330 West Olive Street, Suite 100
Milwaukee, WI 53212 USA

Copyright © 2006 by Weekly Reader® Early Learning Library

Managing Editor: Valerie J. Weber
Editor: Barbara Kiely Miller
Art direction: Tammy West
Graphic design: Dave Kowalski
Photo research: Diane Laska-Swanke

Photo credits: Cover, title, pp. 4, 18 © James P. Rowan; pp. 5, 13 Dave Kowalski/© Weekly Reader Early
Learning Library, 2006; pp. 6, 15, 17 © Ira Block/National Geographic/Getty Images; pp. 7, 8 © Kean
Collection/Getty Images; pp. 9, 11 © MPI/Getty Images; pp. 10, 12 © North Wind Picture Archives;
p. 14 © Eugene G. Schulz; pp. 16, 19, 21 © Pat & Chuck Blackley

All rights reserved. No part of this book may be reproduced, stored in a retrieval system,
or transmitted in any form or by any means, electronic, mechanical, photocopying, recording,
or otherwise, without the prior written permission of the copyright holder.

Printed in the United States of America

1 2 3 4 5 6 7 8 9 10 09 08 07 06

Table of Contents

Copies of the colonists' ships, including the *Godspeed* (*center*) and *Discovery* (*right*), are docked in Jamestown.

A Settlement in Virginia

In 1607, about one hundred men and boys sailed in three ships from England. They landed on North America's eastern coast. They came to search for gold and silver. They began Jamestown, the first lasting English settlement in North America. A settlement is a small village.

The men picked swampy land on the bank of the James River. It was near the coast of what is now Virginia. The men named the river and settlement after James I, the king of England.

This map shows the borders of today's states. The colonists built a settlement on the James River in today's Virginia.

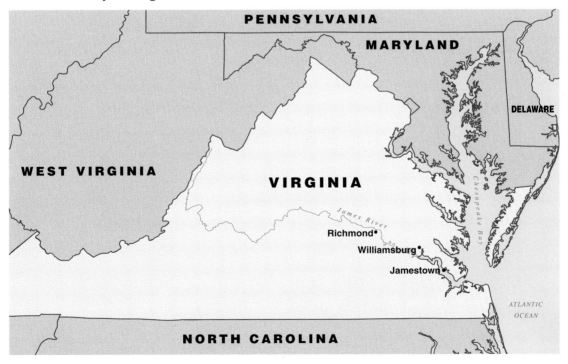

The graves and bones of some early settlers have been found in Jamestown.

First, the settlers built a wooden fort. Then, they built houses, a church, and a building for supplies.

There were problems, though. The settlers could not find enough fresh water to drink. They had trouble growing food and did not know how to hunt. Many people became sick. Others starved. By the end of the summer, half the settlers had died.

Ten thousand Native Americans also lived near the James River. They lived in two hundred villages. These Powhatan Indians did not want settlers on their land. Some of them attacked the settlers.

The English settlers tried to be friends with the Powhatans. They gave gifts to the Powhatan chief.

Captain John Smith told others the story of how Pocahontas saved his life.

A Girl Named Pocahontas

Captain John Smith led the settlers. Hoping to end the fighting, he visited the Powhatan chief. He also wanted to trade for food. The chief's guards grabbed Smith. They might have killed him, but the chief's twelve-year-old daughter saved his life. Pocahontas wrapped her arms around Smith's head. She also helped the settlers and the Powhatans to get along.

More people moved to Jamestown from England. One of them was John Rolfe. He married Pocahontas. There was no gold and silver, so the settlers needed to earn money. In 1612, Rolfe learned from the Powhatans how to grow tobacco. He sold it in England. More settlers began to grow tobacco in Virginia.

Pocahontas visited England with her husband, John Rolfe. Many years later, this portrait was painted of her.

The first Africans came to Jamestown on Dutch ships.

The Start of Slavery and a New Government

In 1619, people from Africa came to Jamestown for the first time. The settlers made them work in the tobacco fields. Later, ships brought thousands of other Africans to Jamestown. The Africans had to work hard and were not paid. They had no freedom. They were slaves. Jamestown is the place where slavery started in the United States.

Settlers from Jamestown began to spread out. They started ten new settlements in the colony of Virginia. In 1619, the colony formed a new government. For the first time, colonists could choose their own leaders. Men in each settlement voted for two people to make decisions for them in the government. The group of men elected helped make the laws. This is the same kind of government we have today.

The elected representatives met in Jamestown for the first time on July 30, 1619.

© North Wind Picture Archives

Angry farmers wanted to take more land from the Natives. They burned the buildings in Jamestown.

The government met in Jamestown. In 1676, some angry tobacco farmers did not agree with the government. They burned down Jamestown. The settlement was rebuilt. One year later, the statehouse burned again. In 1699, the center of government, or capital, moved to Williamsburg.

The colony of Virginia grew larger. It was one of thirteen colonies that were ruled by England. The colonies declared their freedom in 1776. They formed the United States of America. In 1788, Virginia became the tenth state in the country.

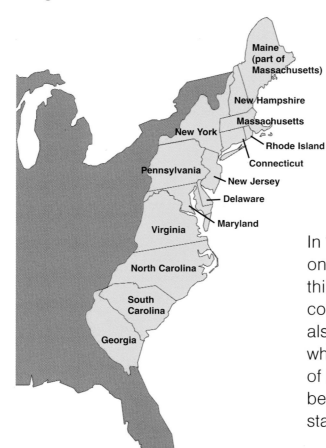

In 1776, Virginia was one of the nation's thirteen original colonies. This map also includes Maine, which was then part of Massachusetts. It became a separate state in 1820.

The ruins of some Jamestown buildings still stand.

Saving Jamestown

The James River flooded Jamestown many times. The floods turned Jamestown into an island. Homes, buildings, and farms were destroyed. The people left Jamestown to live in other places.

In 1893, a group of people in Virginia bought part of Jamestown Island. They wanted to save the buildings that still stood. In 1934, the National Park Service bought the rest of the island. The two groups worked together to save Jamestown's buildings and history.

Ruins of the fort built in early Jamestown were dug up along the shore of Jamestown Island.

Since 1901, people have been digging to uncover pieces of the Jamestown settlement.

Archeologists study how people in the past lived. They looked for what the Jamestown settlers had left behind. They discovered the basements of homes and other buildings. The buildings dated back to 1610.

The archeologists found many items that belonged to the settlers. They dug up clay tobacco pipes, bottles, cooking pots, and window glass. They uncovered parts of guns and swords. They found nails, combs, and rings.

Archeologists have dug up more than 350,000 items left in Jamestown by the colonists.

This Indian lodge was built to look like it did in the 1600s. It is part of a rebuilt Powhatan village.

Visiting Jamestown

Today, the Jamestown Settlement is open to visitors. The digging and other work are not finished. The settlement is being recreated, or rebuilt. It will look like it did during colonial times. A Powhatan village has also been rebuilt with houses, a garden, and a circle for dances. A statue of Pocahontas honors her help to the settlers.

The settlers' fort has been recreated, too. Inside its walls stand houses, a church, and a storehouse. Visitors can help plant gardens or cook meals. The three ships the first settlers used have also been recreated. Visitors can learn what it was like to make the long journey from England.

People dressed as colonists show visitors what life was like in the Jamestown settlement.

Jamestown Facts:
What Archeologists Have Found

Bones that show the colonists ate fish and birds. They also ate raccoons, snakes, and turtles.

Blue glass beads and copper metal beads from England. Settlers used the beads to trade with the Powhatans.

Pieces of cooking dishes and pots the Powhatans used to bring corn to the settlers.

Glass bottles and pieces of glass made at the settlement's glasshouse. Built in 1608, it also made drinking glasses and windows. The glasshouse was America's first factory.

More than one million people come to Jamestown Island each year. Jamestown's four-hundredth birthday is in 2007. People who visit learn about the importance of the settlement. The settlers did not find the gold and silver they came looking for. Instead, they helped start a new country.

This church tower is the only building from the 1600s still standing in Jamestown. It is one of the oldest buildings built by the English in the United States.

Glossary

archeologists — people who study how people lived in the past

colony — a place that is controlled by a government in another country

fort — an area or building made stronger to protect against attacks. Walls usually surround forts.

recreate — to build something again to make it look like it used to

representatives — people who are elected or chosen to act for others

settlement — a small community in a new place; an area where a group of people live together

slaves — people who are owned by other people and made to work without pay. They are not free.

slavery — when people are not free, are owned as property, and are made to work without pay

statehouse — the building where an elected state government meets

For More Information

Books

Captain John Smith. Discover the Life of an Explorer (series). Trish Kline (Rourke Publishing)

The Colony of Virginia. The Thirteen Colonies and The Lost Colony (series). Brooke Coleman (PowerKids Press)

Pocahontas. Compass Point Early Biographies (series). Lucia Raatma (Compass Point Books)

The Powhatan People. Native People (series). Covert, Kim (Capstone Press)

Web Sites

The Jamestown Online Adventure
www.historyglobe.com/jamestown
Make the decisions for the Jamestown Settlement. See if you can do better than the real colonists.

Jamestown Rediscovery
www.apva.org/cereal.htm
Learn about the items and buildings discovered on Jamestown Island.

Index

About the Author

Frances E. Ruffin has written more than twenty-four books for children. She enjoys reading and writing about the lives of famous and ordinary people. She lives in New York City with her son, Timothy, a young writer who is writing his first novel.